EYE TO EYE WITH DOGS

MUTTS

Lynn M. Stone

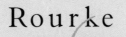

Rourke
Publishing LLC
Vero Beach, Florida 32964

www.rourkepublishing.com

PHOTO CREDITS: All photos © Lynn M. Stone; except p. 17 © Boros Emese

Editor: Meg Greve

Cover and page design by Nicola Stratford

Library of Congress Cataloging-in-Publication Data

Stone, Lynn M.
 Mutts / Lynn M. Stone.
    p. cm. -- (Eye to eye with dogs)
 Includes index.
 ISBN 978-1-60472-364-9
 1. Mutts (Dogs)--Juvenile literature. I. Title.
 SF426.5.S76 2009
 636.7--dc22
                                    2008012978

Rourke Publishing
Printed in the United States of America, North Mankato, Minnesota
011310
011310LP

Rourke Publishing

www.rourkepublishing.com – rourke@rourkepublishing.com
Post Office Box 3328, Vero Beach, FL 32964

Table of Contents

This golden retriever pup, a purebred, will grow up to look like both parents.

Mutts

Mutts are dogs that are not purebreds. A purebred dog is one whose parents are both from the same **breed**. A golden retriever mother and golden retriever father, for example, will have purebred golden retriever pups.

MUTT FACTS
Weight: any
Height: any
Country of Origin: all
Life Span: about 13 years

A mutt can be a mixture of two breeds or of many breeds. Many people call mutts mongrels, mixed breeds, or crossbreeds.

A mutt can be any mix of breeds, such as this cross between a German shepherd and a border collie.

Native Americans developed the purebred Alaskan malamute hundreds of years ago.

For many hundreds of years most dogs were mixes of one kind or another. They could be any shape, any size, and any **temperament**. Some dogs, though, were more useful and attractive than others.

People learned that by carefully selecting parent dogs with the same qualities, they could produce pups with the parents' qualities. By handpicking dog parents, people developed purebreds.

Scottish hunters eventually developed the golden retriever to satisfy their desires for a new breed.

More than 100 years ago, for example, Scottish bird hunters wanted a special type of dog. They wanted an attractive, medium-sized retrieving dog with a light tan or cream coat.

Over several years, they probably mixed bloodhound, Tweed water spaniel, and Irish setter, among other breeds. The hunters' efforts resulted in the golden retriever.

Modern dog **breeders** create some crossbreed, or hybrid, dogs on purpose. Sometimes called designer dogs, breeders designed them for a reason, such as excellent hunting skills or a sweet disposition.

The Labradoodle is the best known of recent designer dogs.

Australian Wally Conron began to develop the Labradoodle by crossing a Lab with a standard poodle.

The Labradoodle, for example, is a **cross** between a Labrador retriever and a poodle. Breeders designed the Labradoodle to be a guide dog that did not shed. Intentional crosses, however, do not always result in dogs with the qualities the breeder wants.

Looks

A mutt may be unique, or different from all others. A mutt pup's looks depend upon its parents. It may have a mixed breed parent and a purebred parent. It may have two purebred parents of different breeds. It may have two mixed breed parents. The possibilities are endless!

The owners of this handsome mutt know its ancestors were a German shepherd dog and a Catahoula hound.

Mutts range in size from tiny to large.

A mixed breed dog may be any color, or combination of colors, known to dogs. Its hair can be straight or curly, long or short. Mutts can also have almost any body shape.

Mutts of the Past

The earliest dog breeds probably date back some 15,000 years. People then, and for generations afterward, made little effort to develop purebreds. Until recently, nearly all dogs were mutts.

Mutts have been around since people first began to develop the dog, perhaps as many as 15,000 years ago.

The Dog for You?

Raise any dog with love and care and you will probably have a good dog. It does not matter whether it is a mutt or a purebred. After all, no dogs possess the wild temperament of wolves, the dog's earliest **ancestors**.

Mutts are just as loveable as their purebred cousins.

Two English springer spaniel parents are likely to have pups that act and look just like them.

One argument in favor of a purebred dog is its **predictability**. Usually, a purebred pup will grow up to look and act like its mom and dad.

The German shorthaired pointer is a prized hunting dog.

For example, someone who wants a bird hunting dog will choose a breed that has great **instincts** to find or retrieve birds. Taking a dog with unknown ancestors would not be a good choice for a hunter.

People may want a dog for a special look, like the bulldog's wrinkly face, or they may want a reliably good-natured dog, like the Labrador.

The Lab's temperament has helped make it the most popular dog in North America for many years.

Dog owners love the bulldog for its unusual muzzle.

There are advantages to purebreds. There are also advantages to mutts. One advantage to owning a mutt is cost. Most mixed breed dogs are not expensive.

Mutts are far less expensive than purebreds.

Irish setters are prone to blindness. Breeders use a test to make sure that both parents do not have this disease before breeding them.

However, perhaps a better reason to consider a mutt, is the dog's health. Dogs pass diseases to one another through their parents.

Certain purebreds tend to carry certain conditions or diseases, such as arthritis. Crossing a purebred with a different breed or mixed breed reduces the chance of passing diseases from parents to pups.

Dog experts call this improvement in health *hybrid vigor*. Hybrid is another name for a cross between two breeds. Vigor refers to health and strength.

This mixed breed dog has a better chance of being healthier than its purebred ancestors.

Mutts can compete with purebreds in contests of agility and obedience.

Mutts can be as talented as purebreds in contests of **agility**, obedience, and athletics, like Frisbee and fly ball. If you get a mutt pup, you will have to wait to see what talents and temperament the dog will show as it grows up.

A Note about Dogs

Puppies are cute and cuddly, but only after serious thought should anybody buy one. Puppies, after all, grow up.

A dog will require more than love and patience. It will need healthy food, exercise, grooming, medical care, and a warm, safe place to live.

A dog can be your best friend, but you need to be its best friend, too.

Choosing the right breed for you requires homework. For more information about buying and owning a dog, contact the American Kennel Club or the Canadian Kennel Club.

Glossary

agility (AJ-il-itee): the ability to perform certain athletic tasks, such as leaping through a hoop

ancestors (AN-sess-turz): animals that at some time in the past were part of the modern animal's family

breed (BREED): a particular kind of domestic animal within a larger, closely related group, such as the golden retriever within the dog group

breeders (BREED-urz): those who keep adult dogs and raise their pups, especially those who do so regularly and with great care

cross (KRAWS): to match parents together, or the offspring that result from a match of different breeds

instincts (IN-stingkt): the abilities and desires with which an animal is born, not taught

predictability (pri-DIKT-uh-bil-itee): the level of certainty in a situation

temperament (TEM-pur-uh-muhnt): how an animal behaves, such as being affectionate or loyal

Index

Further Reading

King, Stephen Michael. *Mutt Dog*. Scholastic, 2005.
Murray, Julie. *Mutts*. Buddy Books, 2002.
Rake, Jody Sullivan. *Mutts*. Pebble Books, 2007.

Website to Visit

ndrc.tripod.com/areyou.htm
www.crossbreed-and-mongrel-club.org.uk
http://www.web.ukonline.co.uk/k9z.uk/about.html

About the Author

Lynn M. Stone is a widely-published wildlife and domestic animal photographer and the author of more than 500 children's books. His book *Box Turtles* was chosen as an Outstanding Science Trade Book and Selectors' Choice for 2008 by the Science Committee of the National Science Teachers' Association and the Children's Book Council.